HERE COMES THE SUN

A *Hi and Lois* Collection by Mort Walker and Dik Browne

A *King Features* COMIC

AVON BOOKS ▲ NEW YORK

W9-BSA-311

HERE COMES THE SUN is an original publication of Avon Books. This work has never before appeared in book form.

AVON BOOKS
A Division of
The Hearst Corporation
105 Madison Avenue
New York, NY 10016

Cover design by Bob Browne and Frank Caruso
Flip book drawings by Bob Browne
Interior editing and design by Brian Walker

First Avon Books Trade Printing: May 1990

AVON TRADEMARK REG. U.S. PAT. OFF. AND IN OTHER COUNTRIES, MARCA REGISTRADA, HECHO EN U.S.A.

Printed in the U.S.A.

CW 10 9 8 7 6 5 4 3 2 1

THE EXTENDED FAMILY

The roots of the "Hi and Lois" family tree go back to 1954. "Beetle Bailey" creator Mort Walker was concerned that the success of his new army comic strip, which began in 1950, would fade after the end of the Korean War. As an experiment, he sent Beetle home on leave to visit his sister, Lois. While Beetle pondered his future, readers wrote in demanding his return to the military. Sylvan Byck, the comics editor of King Features Syndicate suggested to Mort that he create a new feature centered around Beetle's sister and her family. Since Mort already had three children at home (with four more to follow) he could draw on his own personal experiences. Mort liked the idea, provided he could find an artist to illustrate the strip. Sylvan and Mort each came up with the names of prospective candidates and Dik Browne, a talented advertising cartoonist, who was also a devoted family man, was at the top of both lists. Mort and Dik hit it off immediately and one of the legendary partnerships in comics history began.

After its debut in 1954, "Hi and Lois" grew slowly but steadily in popularity. Circulation finally began to climb more dramatically in the early 1960's when Trixie, the

youngest member of the Flagston clan, blossomed. Readers delighted in looking at the world through Trixie's eyes and fell in love with her precocious charm. "Hi and Lois" was voted the best humor strip by the National Cartoonists Society in 1959 and 1960 and Dik Browne was presented with the prestigious Reuben Award as the "best cartoonist of the year" in 1962.

The "Hi and Lois" creative family also grew during the 50's and 60's as Jerry Dumas, Bob Gustafson and Bud Jones joined the writing staff. This gifted group helped come up with ideas for Mort's many comic creations and enjoyed golf, bowling, ping pong and each other's company.

From the baby boom years, through the turbulent Sixties and on into the Me Decade, "Hi and Lois" reflected the changing fads and fashions of American society while lampooning the unchanging realities of family life. Coonskin caps, hula hoops, Beatle wigs, hippie beads and disco records came and went but teddy bears, peanut butter sandwiches, baseball cards and doll houses remained. The Flagston household survived as an oasis of normalcy in an increasingly perplexing world.

In the 1980's the creative challenge of producing "Hi and Lois" was handed down to the next generation. Bob

Browne, Brian Walker and Greg Walker, all of whom grew up reading their own childhood exploits in the panels of "Hi and Lois", now find themselves continuing the family legacy. They currently have seven children between them and bring their own perspectives to the strip. Without missing a step, the Flagstons now confront the modern problems of day care, dual careers and diaper disposal as the baby boom generation goes beyond thirtysomething.

To many, "Hi and Lois" has been more than just a comic strip. It has provided a common link between the Walker and Browne families for four decades and has bound together a close knit fraternity of cartoonists, affectionately known as "King Features East". It has also drawn the readers into the fold. A fan once wrote that she felt like the "Hi and Lois" creators were looking into the window of her home when she read the strip. This is the key to the success of "Hi and Lois". It doesn't have to be side-splitting every day but it must be consistently true to life, reflecting the daily concerns of its readers. "Hi and Lois" deals with common experiences that are shared by millions. This book is dedicated to the parents, grandparents and kids all over the world who have become an important part of the "Hi and Lois" extended family.

ACKNOWLEDGMENTS

"Hi and Lois" was launched on October 18th, 1954 with Mort Walker as the writer and Dik Browne as the artist. Fred Schwartz, a veteran of the King Features bullpen has lettered the strip since its inception. Jerry Dumas began submitting ideas to "Hi and Lois" in 1956, Bob Gustafson came aboard in 1962 and Bud Jones rounded out the writing staff in 1968. Frank Johnson took over the inking from Dik Browne in the early 1970's and continues that duty today. Bob Browne, who started assisting his Dad with the drawing of the strip in 1980 has taken over full-time since Dik's passing in 1989. Mort's oldest son, Greg, first submitted gags to "Hi and Lois" in the early 1970's and is still writing today. Another of Mort's sons, Brian, contributed his first ideas in 1984 and is now the chief writer and editor of "Hi and Lois". This book contains work by all of these talented artists and writers.

FLIP ME

GOSH, THIS NEWS IS DEPRESSING! MAKES YOU WONDER WHETHER THE WORLD HAS A FUTURE
SOMETIMES I FEEL LIKE THAT FOR A WHILE
WHAT DO YOU DO?
DIK BROWNE 4-10
© 1989 King Features Syndicate, Inc. World rights reserved.
WATCH TRIXIE FOR A FEW MINUTES
HEE HEE HEE

I LOVE YOU, TRIXIE
I LOVE YOU, TOO, TRIXIE
DIK BROWNE
I'D BETTER ENJOY THIS WHILE I CAN
© 1989 King Features Syndicate, Inc. World rights reserved
IN A FEW SECONDS THEY'LL BE FIGHTING OVER WHO LOVES ME MORE
12-27

HEY, SUNSHINE, CAN YOU TURN IT DOWN A LITTLE?
© 1988 King Features Syndicate, Inc. World rights reserved
MOM JUST CLEANED IN HERE AND YOU'RE MAKING HER LOOK BAD!
2-17
DIK BROWNE

COULD YOU DO ME A FAVOR, MISTER MOONBEAM?
© 1989 King Features Syndicate, Inc. World rights reserved
TELL YOUR FRIEND THE SUNBEAM I'D LIKE TO SEE HIM IN THE MORNING
DIK BROWNE
7-12

HEY, TRIXIE! DID YOU KNOW THAT A SHORT WHILE AGO YOU WERE INSIDE MOM'S TUMMY?

BETCHA DIDN'T KNOW THAT!

HA HA HA!! TELL ME ANOTHER ONE!!

I DON'T CARE WHAT THEY SAY, BIG SISTERS ARE FUN!

DIK BROWNE 9-17

WHAT ARE WE HAVING FOR DINNER?

SKETTI

IT'S NOT SKETTI, IT'S PUH-SKETTI

WELL, YOU LEARN SOMETHING NEW EVERY DAY

I THOUGHT IT WAS SCUPETTI

DIK BROWNE

12-13

WE CAN'T DECIDE. YOU'RE THE PROFESSIONAL—WHY DO **YOU** THINK WE SHOULD BUY THIS HOUSE?
IT HAS LARGE ROOMS, A TWO-CAR GARAGE, IT'S CLOSE TO SHOPPING, AND MY DAUGHTER NEEDS BRACES FOR HER TEETH
DIK BROWNE
2-3
© 1987 King Features Syndicate, Inc. World rights reserved.
AT LAST, A REAL ESTATE AGENT WHO TELLS IT LIKE IT IS!

HERE'S A NICE HOUSE WITH THREE FIREPLACES AND A NEW FURNACE
DIDN'T WE SEE THAT HOUSE LAST SUMMER?
YEH
© 1987 King Features Syndicate, Inc. World rights reserved.
ONLY THEN IT WAS A NICE HOUSE WITH A POOL AND CENTRAL AIR CONDITIONING
12-29
DIK BROWNE

YOU LOOK AS PRETTY AS THE DAY WE GOT MARRIED
© 1989 King Features Syndicate, Inc. World rights reserved
BEFORE OR AFTER YOU SHOVED THE WEDDING CAKE IN MY FACE?
DIK BROWNE
8-28

LOOK AT HOW YOUNG YOU LOOK IN THIS PICTURE, MOM! WHEN WAS IT TAKEN?
OH, ABOUT 2 B.C.
PHOTOS
© 1988 King Features Syndicate, Inc. World rights reserved
WHAT DO YOU MEAN?
TWO YEARS BEFORE CHILDREN
PHOTOS
2-5
DIK BROWNE

I NEED PEACE AND QUIET! DOES ANYONE AROUND HERE KNOW WHAT THAT IS?
© 1987 King Features Syndicate, Inc. World rights reserved.
SURE, THAT'S WHAT YOU FIND IN A HOUSE WITHOUT CHILDREN
WAAA!
DIK BROWNE 11-16

DITTO WANTS TO PLAY CATCH, DEAR
WHY DON'T YOU PLAY WITH HIM?
THERE'S NO REASON A MOTHER CAN'T PLAY CATCH WITH HER SON
OK, FINE
DIK BROWNE 9-12
© 1988 King Features Syndicate, Inc. World rights reserved
YOU PLAY DOLLS WITH DOT

THE PLUMBER CAME WHILE YOU WERE OUT
OH? WHAT DID HE SAY?
$275
© 1988 King Features Syndicate, Inc. World rights reserved
DIK BROWNE
2-6

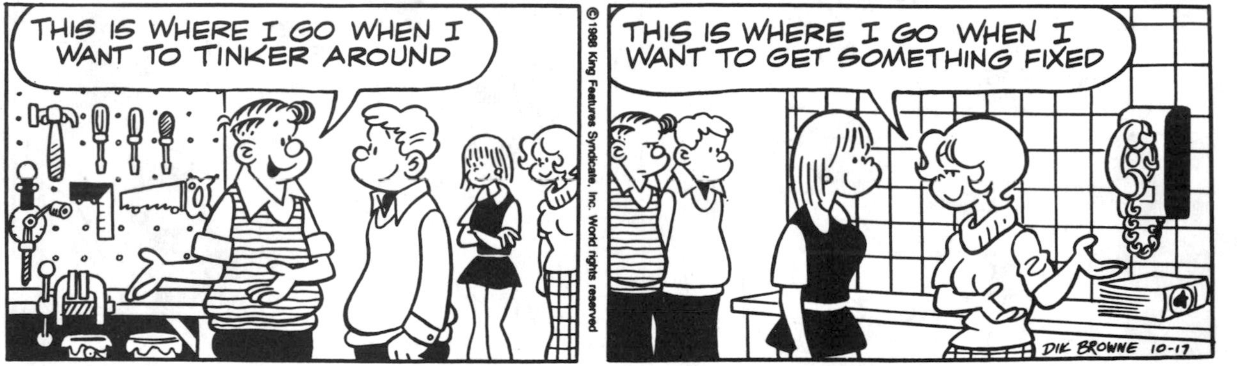
THIS IS WHERE I GO WHEN I WANT TO TINKER AROUND
© 1988 King Features Syndicate, Inc. World rights reserved
THIS IS WHERE I GO WHEN I WANT TO GET SOMETHING FIXED
DIK BROWNE 10-17

THE KIDS ARE FED, THE DISHES ARE DONE AND THE KITCHEN IS CLEAN
YOU'RE DOING SUCH A GOOD JOB
I'M NOT NEEDED ANYMORE!
©1986 King Features Syndicate, Inc. World rights reserved.
I DIDN'T REALIZE YOU CAN BECOME **TOO**-WELL HOUSE-TRAINED
DIK BROWNE
9-16

WHAT ARE YOU DOING HERE, MR. FLAGSTON?
YOU'RE NOT OUT OF WORK, ARE YOU?
©1986 King Features Syndicate, Inc. World rights reserved.
I'M BUYING FOOD FOR MY FAMILY! **THAT'S WORKING**, ISN'T IT? ISN'T HOUSEWORK CONSIDERED WORK?!
HIS WIFE MUST BE WORKING
11-29
DIK BROWNE

HOW'S IT GOING, DEAR ?
I JUST FIGURED OUT WHAT INFLATION IS ALL ABOUT
WHAT?
FEELING LIKE A MILLION WHEN YOU JUST MANAGED TO SAVE A HUNDRED
DIK BROWNE 6-20
© 1988 King Features Syndicate, Inc. World rights reserved

SINCE LOIS HAS BEEN WORKING, WE'VE BEEN ABLE TO AFFORD A LOT OF THINGS WE COULDN'T AFFORD BEFORE
LIKE WHAT?
FOOD, CLOTHING, SHELTER...
DIK BROWNE 5-12
© 1987 King Features Syndicate, Inc. World rights reserved.

HOW MANY PEOPLE CALLED IN SICK TODAY?

FOOFRAM INDUSTRIES

DIK 5-16 BROWNE

ABOUT THREE FOURSOMES' WORTH

I'M SORRY TO BOTHER YOU, HI, BUT THE PLUMBER WANTS $450 TO REPLACE THOSE PIPES IN THE CELLAR

THAT'S AN OUTRAGEOUS PRICE! I'LL FIND SOMEONE ELSE TO DO THE JOB!

I LIKE THE WAY FLAGSTON SAVES MONEY FOR THE COMPANY

9-29

DIK BROWNE

MAYBE IT IS TOO COLD TO PLAY TODAY
WHY DO YOU SAY THAT?
MY BALL JUST CRACKED IN HALF
DIK BROWNE 1-31

IT SURE HAS BEEN A LONG, COLD WINTER
THEY SAY WE'RE ENTERING A NEW ICE AGE
IT COULD BE THE BEGINNING OF THE END OF GOLF AS WE KNOW IT
DIK BROWNE 2-25

I HATE SUMMER! ALL THIS GRASS!
HOW ABOUT WINTER? ALL THAT SNOW?
8-12
HOW ABOUT FALL?... ALL THOSE LEAVES AND IN SPRING YOU TOOK OFF THE STORM WINDOWS... WASHED THEM, WASHED THE REGULAR WINDOWS...
DIK BROWNE
© 1987 King Features Syndicate, Inc. World rights reserved.
...AND CLEANED OUT THE BASEMENT, THE GARAGE...
I HATE LITTLE BROTHERS!

DO YOU LOVE US, CHIP?
I GUESS SO
DIK BROWNE
© 1988 King Features Syndicate, Inc. World rights reserved
3-4
BUT YOU'LL NEVER CATCH ME SHOWING IT!

GOING TO THE BEACH IS ALWAYS A BIG DISAPPOINTMENT
WHY?
THE GIRLS NEVER LOOK AS GOOD AS THEY DO IN "SPORTS ILLUSTRATED"
DIK BROWNE 6-4
© 1988 King Features Syndicate, Inc. World rights reserved

DAD, CAN YOU TELL ME SOME MORE FACTS OF LIFE?
WHY?
SO I'LL HAVE SOME MORE FUNNY STORIES TO TELL MY SEX-EDUCATION CLASS
DIK BROWNE 3-6
© 1987 King Features Syndicate, Inc. World rights reserved.

FROM NOW ON THE TV STAYS OFF DURING DINNER, WE'RE GOING TO TALK FOR A CHANGE
© 1988 King Features Syndicate, Inc. World rights reserved
DIK BROWNE 1-11
HAS ANYBODY GOT ANYTHING TO SAY?
I'M WATCHING WHEEL OF FORTUNE AFTER DINNER
NO, YOU'RE NOT! THERE'S A GAME ON!
HEY! I'M WATCHING CARTOONS!

WHEN I WAS A KID WE HAD TO WEAR A TIE TO DINNER
AND WE COULDN'T LEAVE THE TABLE UNTIL WE WERE EXCUSED
DIK BROWNE
5-2
© 1988 King Features Syndicate, Inc. World rights reserved
I GUESS TV SAVED **US** FROM ALL THAT, HUH?

LET'S SEE, WHICH PACIFIER DO I WANT TO USE TODAY? I JUST CAN'T MAKE UP MY MIND
7-2
TRIXIE!!
DIK BROWNE
© 1988 King Features Syndicate, Inc. World rights reserved

TIME FOR LUNCH, TRIXIE!
ALREADY?
DIK BROWNE
2-25
© 1987 King Features Syndicate Inc. World rights reserved.
TIME SURE FLIES WHEN YOU'RE PULLING OUT SHOESTRINGS!

YOU'RE THE GREATEST DAD IN THE WHOLE-WIDE WORLD
GEE, THANKS..
COURSE, YOU'RE THE ONLY ONE I KNOW UP CLOSE AND PERSONAL
11-26
DIK BROWNE
© 1987 King Features Syndicate, Inc. World rights reserved.

PRESS

YOU USED TO GET BETTER GRADES THAN THIS, DITTO. WHAT HAPPENED?
REPORT CARD
DIK BROWNE 11/17
I PEAKED EARLY
REPORT CARD
© 1988 King Features Syndicate, Inc. World rights reserved

THE DOCTOR GIVES US **LOLLIPOPS!**

DIK BROWNE
5·11

AFTER ALL YOU'VE PUT ME THROUGH YOU OWE ME SOMETHING BETTER THAN A **TOOTHBRUSH**

LOOK AT MY TEETH, DAD!

AND HE PROMISED THE DENTIST HE'D KEEP THEM CLEAN

DIK BROWNE

7-25

DITTO, YOU HAVE TO EAT **SOMETIME**

I'VE NEVER SEEN THAT BOY BE SO STILL FOR SO LONG
WHAT'S HE DOING?
© 1988 King Features Syndicate, Inc. World rights reserved
TRYING TO GET A SQUIRREL TO EAT OFF HIS STOMACH
5-30
DIK BROWNE

WHY DIDN'T YOU EAT YOUR LUNCH?
IT WAS ALL SOGGY
HOW DID THAT HAPPEN?
DIK BROWNE 6·23
© 1988 King Features Syndicate, Inc. World rights reserved
CROAK
I FORGOT TO DRY MY FROG OFF BEFORE I PUT HIM IN MY LUNCH-BOX

DITTO, WHAT ARE YOU DOING WITH THE TOASTER OUTSIDE?!
I KNEW YOU DIDN'T WANT ME SKEET SHOOTING IN THE HOUSE
10/16
DIK BROWNE
© 1987 King Features Syndicate, Inc. World rights reserved.

DAD, CAN YOU HELP ME GET MY KITE?
WHAT HAPPENED TO IT?
IT GOT TANGLED IN THE TELEPHONE-REPAIR MAN
9-25
DIK BROWNE
© 1987 King Features Syndicate, Inc. World rights reserved.

MOM! I CAN'T FIND ANYTHING TO WEAR!
OH, DITTO, HAVE YOU REALLY LOOKED?
YES!
I DON'T BELIEVE YOU **REALLY** LOOKED
© 1986 King Features Syndicate, Inc. World rights reserved.
NOW DO YOU BELIEVE ME?
DIK BROWNE
7-10

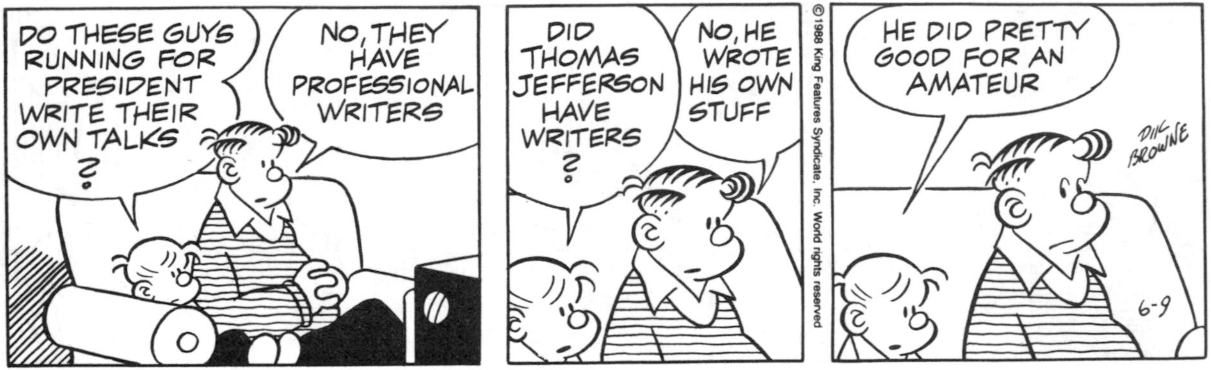

DO THESE GUYS RUNNING FOR PRESIDENT WRITE THEIR OWN TALKS?
NO, THEY HAVE PROFESSIONAL WRITERS
DID THOMAS JEFFERSON HAVE WRITERS?
NO, HE WROTE HIS OWN STUFF
© 1988 King Features Syndicate, Inc. World rights reserved
HE DID PRETTY GOOD FOR AN AMATEUR
DIK BROWNE
6-9

YOU'RE OLD ENOUGH TO KNOW YOU SHOULDN'T DRAW ON THE WALL, DITTO. WHY DID YOU DO IT?
Z
© 1988 King Features Syndicate, Inc. World rights reserved
IT SEEMED LIKE A GOOD IDEA AT THE TIME
Z
DIK BROWNE 11-24

THERE SHOULD BE SOMETHING WE CAN DO WITH THOSE DOTS TRIXIE DREW ON THE WALL, DITTO
1-23
© 1987 King Features Syndicate, Inc. World rights reserved.
I ALREADY DID SOMETHING WITH THEM, DAD
DIK BROWNE

DADDY'S **HOME**!
IT SURE IS NICE TO COME HOME TO OPEN ARMS
EVEN IF THEY ARE COVERED WITH PEANUT BUTTER AND FINGER-PAINT
DIK BROWNE
© 1988 King Features Syndicate, Inc. World rights reserved
5-23

I HAD ANOTHER ONE OF THOSE DAYS AGAIN
TOMORROW'S ANOTHER DAY
8-13
DIK BROWNE
THAT'S WHAT I SAID YESTERDAY!
© 1987 King Features Syndicate, Inc. World rights reserved.

WHAT IS THE THING YOU WOULD WANT THE VERY MOST, MOM?
I SUPPOSE IT WOULD BE WORLD PEACE, LOVE AND UNDERSTANDING
© 1988 King Features Syndicate, Inc. World rights reserved
I GOT DAD'S AND CHIP'S LISTS. DID YOU GET MOM'S CHRISTMAS LIST?
YEAH... AND BOY ARE WE GONNA HAVE A TOUGH TIME SHOPPING
BROWNE
12-8

I FINISHED MY CHRISTMAS LIST
GOOD JOB, DITTO
DIK BROWNE
12-14
© 1989 King Features Syndicate, Inc. World rights reserved
CAN YOU TAKE IT TO THE OFFICE AND FAX IT TO SANTA?